16th June '16.

To Uncle Eric

Happy Birthday!

All our love

Nick Josh Jacques

& Izzy xx.

SOMERSET
COUNTY CRICKET CLUB
The Return to Glory
2001-2007

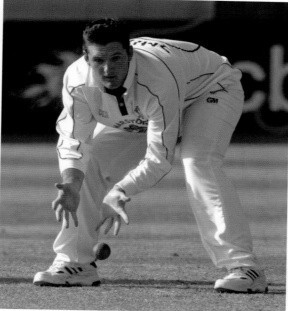

ALAIN LOCKYER

WITH TEXT BY RICHARD WALSH

HALSGROVE

First published in Great Britain in 2015

ISBN 978 0 85704 236 1

HALSGROVE
Halsgrove House,
Ryelands Business Park,
Bagley Road, Wellington, Somerset TA21 9PZ
Tel: 01823 653777   Fax: 01823 216796
email: sales@halsgrove.com

Part of the Halsgrove group of companies.
Information on all Halsgrove titles is available at: www.halsgrove.com

Printed in China by Everbest Printing Co Ltd

Contents

Foreword

by Marcus Trescothick, the Captain of Somerset CCC

I AM DELIGHTED to be able to write the foreword for this book which covers Somerset County Cricket Club between 2001 and 2007, which include our two most recent cup winning seasons, and gaining promoton back to Division One of the championship.

As a player it is always a very special memory to be part of a team that wins a trophy, especially when it is for your own county.

To lift the trophy at the end of all the hard work that you put into a campaign is like a dream come true and it has happened to me twice so far since I started playing at the County Ground.

Back in 2001 we had a good campaign throughout and although I didn't play in the first match at March against Cambridgeshire, we won thanks to a century from Mark Lathwell.

In the next match against Glamorgan at Taunton I made 121 to help us win by seven wickets, which won me the Man of the Match Award. Matt Maynard, who is now our Director of Cricket played in that game and scored 93 not out as well as keeping wicket.

We then beat Kent at home in the quarter final before hosting Warwickshire in the semi final, which we won thanks to a brilliant partnership between Rob Turner and Keith Dutch.

The final was played in front of a packed house at Lord's where we beat Leicestershire to end eighteen years of waiting for our loyal supporters.

By the time we got to 2005 I was a centrally contracted player so missed out on the early T20 matches but I was available to play in the semi-final and final at the Oval and that was another very special occasion.

We had some great players in our team in both of those cup winning sides.

In 2001 Jamie Cox was our captain and he played brilliantly and made a huge impact. Our team was solid throughout the whole campaign and there always seemed to be someone who stood up to help us across the line.

There was a great atmosphere and it was a real team effort that saw us win the Cheltenham & Gloucester Trophy.

In 2005 we had Graeme Smith as our captain and he played a brilliant knock in the final to see us beat Lancashire, who were the favourites, to win us the competition.

He came in as our overseas player and delivered the goods when we were under pressure.

Another great day in 2005 was when Somerset beat Australia in a one day match on 15 June. On that day Graeme Smith and Sanath Jayasuriya both got hundreds and we have got a picture from that game up in the Andy Caddick Pavilion.

I would love to have been a part of that but I was with the England set up by then.

It was great for England because Somerset beat the Australians and then shortly afterwards they lost to Bangladesh at Cardiff in a one day game. We then played them at Bristol the next day and beat them and that became the catalyst for the 2005 Ashes success.

The joy of lifting a trophy is something that you don't get to experience that often but when you do it is a very special moment and I'd love to be able to taste it just one more time before I finish!

Introduction
by Alain Lockyer

I AM DELIGHTED to have been invited by Halsgrove to make a further selection of my pictures to use in this book: *Return to Glory*.

The vast majority of the photographs I have taken over the years have appeared in newspapers and magazines, which after their brief shelf life have inevitably been disposed of, so to see some of them used in a book like this again and reproduced on high quality paper is a real treat.

While the pictures that appeared in my previous book *Somerset Cricket – the Glory Years*, were virtually all in black and white and taken on film, the photographs included in this book are digital images and captured on Nikon cameras using a Nikon or Sigma long lens.

As well as being a professional photographer, having been born and brought up in Taunton I am a real local and a huge Somerset supporter myself. I have shared the ups and downs of the Club since I first started to follow them.

My professional career coincided roughly with the arrival of Ian Botham back in the 1970s and I was fortunate enough to have been able to record Somerset's success during the Glory Years when they won five one day trophies in as many seasons.

Nobody was happier than me when Somerset ended an eighteen-year wait for more silverware and the crowd scenes witnessed during the 2001 Cheltenham & Gloucester Trophy winning campaign were reminiscent of those from the Glory Years – the sheer delight on the players' and fans' faces is clear to see.

One of the biggest problems has been the selection of the images to use in this book, and initially the pictures were chosen on photographic merit and then fitted into a cricketing time frame.

Once again I am indebted to my co-author Richard Walsh who has done all the hard work and without whom this book would not have come to fruition.

Finally I hope you enjoy the contents and let's hope it won't be too long before Somerset win another trophy!

Alain Lockyer
January 2015

Introduction
by Richard Walsh

WHEN IT WAS announced that Somerset had signed Tasmanian top order batsman Jamie Cox to become their captain for the 1999 season, supporters were unsure what to expect as he was little known outside of Australia where he had an impressive record in domestic cricket.

However when Cox did arrive to take up his post ahead of the season, with the fledgling Marcus Trescothick as his number two, it was quickly apparent that Somerset had made another very shrewd signing from Down Under.

The twenty-nine year-old immediately brought that Aussie determination and confidence, yet not in a brash hard nosed way.

Cox was an immediate success and quickly won the hearts of the County Ground faithful who were growing ever hungrier for success. He led Somerset to a very respectable fourth place in the championship and took the county back to Lord's for their first one day final since 1983, although they were beaten by the old foe Gloucestershire.

During that season Cox scored 1617 runs in the championship at 57.75, with six centuries and a best of 216 and was well supported on the batting front by wicket-keeper Rob Turner who hit 1217 at 52.91, Peter Bowler who made 931, Mike Burns 915 and Trescothick 898, which included 197 against Glamorgan in front of future England coach Duncan Fletcher.

On the bowling side Andy Caddick was still in his prime and celebrated his benefit season by taking 71 first class wickets for Somerset at just under 21 runs apiece, while young left arm seamer Matt Bulbeck offered good support with 51 at 28.54.

In 2000 the championship was divided into two divisions, but Cox maintained Somerset's form and they ended fifth in the top flight, even though they won only twice.

The highlight of the campaign was beating West Indies by 269 runs, a victory that included a hat-trick for Jason Kerr and a career best 193 for Keith Parsons.

Bowler topped the county's championship batting averages scoring 1090 runs with four centuries at 57.36, while Ian Blackwell who joined that season from Derbyshire hit his maiden century for his new club.

Leading wicket taker that season was Steffan Jones with 40 wickets.

2001 will go down as one of Somerset's most successful seasons because they ended second in Division One of the championship, their best ever until then, but probably more importantly for their loyal and long-suffering supporters they won the Cheltenham & Gloucester Trophy at Lord's ending the eighteen-year silverware famine.

That success was achieved to a large degree without the services of both Andy Caddick and Marcus

Trescothick who by this time were both centrally contracted for England and was very much an all round team effort, led by their skipper Cox and Kevin Shine, who had taken over from Dermot Reeve as coach.

Somerset had been joined by Middlesex duo Richard Johnson and Keith Dutch, who both played their parts in the team's success.

Johnson took 62 championship wickets at 23.77 to earn himself an England call up, while in addition to his off breaks Dutch scored his maiden century and played a key innings in the C & G semi final against Warwickshire to get Somerset to Lord's.

Cox headed up the Somerset batting with 1264 runs at 57.45, with good support from Blackwell who hit four centuries in his own style, Mike Burns who hit a double century at Bath and Bowler.

Keith Parsons once again proved himself to be a great all-round asset and deservedly won the Man of the Match Award at Lord's, while Jones enjoyed another good season with the ball, taking 59 championship wickets.

After the giddy heights of the previous season 2002 was something of an anti-climax, and although Somerset returned to Lord's to defend the C & G Trophy, where they were beaten by Yorkshire, at the end of the campaign they were relegated in both the championship and the Norwich Union League.

Highspots of the season were 1000 championship runs for Burns, the big hitting of Blackwell who hit three centuries and the performances of Pete Trego who hit a career best 140 in the tied game with West Indies A and Matt Wood who hit 971 four day runs in only his second season.

2003 saw the arrival of the new Twenty20 Cup competition, but Somerset didn't fare particularly well in any form of the game that season.

Most memorable in Burns' first season as captain in place of Cox was the batting of big hitting Blackwell who scored 1066 championship runs including a never to be forgotten unbeaten 247 against his former county Derbyshire, his second ton coming off a mere 41 balls.

Burns and Cox both scored 1000 runs in the season, and there were maiden centuries for Cornishman Neil Edwards and Aaron Laraman, another recruit from Middlesex. while on the bowling side Nixon McLean, who joined from Hampshire took 65 wickets at 28.80.

In 2004 there were a number of individual highlights but generally team performances were disappointing.

James Hildreth announced himself on the scene with a championship century against a strong Durham attack which included Shoaib Akhtar and Neil Killeen.

Australian captain Ricky Ponting played for a brief while and made an instant impression with two championship hundreds in his three matches, which saw him leave with an average of 99.

Cox topped 1000 runs in his final season at Taunton which included 250 at Trent Bridge before heading home to Australia.

In the one day competitions Simon Francis saw Somerset to victory in the second round of the C & G with a remarkable bowling spell that reduced hosts Derbyshire from 216 for three to 276 all out, 14 runs short of their target.

The former Hampshire paceman's figures of eight for 66 from 9.5 overs was a career best and new Somerset record.

Expectations for 2005 were high as soon as it was announced that South African captain Graeme Smith was coming to skipper Somerset and he didn't disappoint, coupled with the early season stint of Sri Lankan run maker Sanath Jayasuriya.

In the championship there were some impressive contributions with Blackwell, Wood and John Francis, who had followed his brother Simon from Hampshire, all topping 1000 runs.

Blackwell enjoyed another fine season with the bat and won the Walter Lawrence Trophy for the fastest century of the season, while Wood enjoyed his best season and fell just short of a triple century in the match against Yorkshire at Taunton.

However it was in the Twenty20 Cup that Somerset excelled, led by a masterful Smith who hit 380 runs in his 11 matches at an average of 38.00. The South African was truly inspirational and under his leadership a largely young Somerset side lifted the T20 Cup for the first time – after a memorable day of cricket at the Oval at the end of July.

But that wasn't all because on 15 June Smith led Somerset to victory over the might of Australia in a 50 over game in front of a packed house at the County Ground.

2006 won't be remembered as one of Somerset's best as they ended bottom of the Division Two table in the championship and failed to qualify for the latter stages in any of the one-day competitions.

However there were some impressive performances from the newly recruited players. Bowler Charl Willoughby signed from Leicestershire took 66 wickets, young Australian Cameron White topped 1000 runs in four day cricket and all rounder Pete Trego returned to his native county and enjoyed a successful year.

Former Australian Test batsman Justin Langer only played a handful of games but set a new Somerset record first class innings score of 342 as well as helping to post a new T20 record total of 250.

Langer returned the following season and led Somerset to promotion back to Division One of the championship and they also lifted themselves back into the top flight in the 40 over competition by finishing second in Division Two.

Four batsmen topped 1000 championship runs in 2007, White, Marcus Trescothick, Langer and James Hildreth.

One bright new face that appeared on the Somerset scene that season was nineteen-year-old South African born Craig Kieswetter a wicket-keeper batsman who took over the 'keeping duties in early May and never looked back.

Langer's achievements in 2007 laid the foundations for Somerset to go on and achieve their best ever finish in the championship three years later when they ended joint top of the table with Nottinghamshire, only to be beaten by the midland county who had won an extra match.

Everybody would love it to be the County Championship that Somerset win next, because that's the only trophy they have never lifted, but failing that supporters would be happy to see their beloved county claim any of the trophies that they compete for each season.

2001
The Cheltenham & Gloucester Trophy Winning Season

Somerset squad in 2001.

Back row, left to right – Ross Dewar, (Second XI Physio), Matt Wood, Tom Webley, Joe Tucker, Steffan Jones, Jason Kerr, Matt Bulbeck, Ian Jones, Carl Gazzard, Chris Hunkin, Arul Suppiah and Darren Veness (First XI Physio).

Middle row, left to right – Andy Hurry (Fitness Instructor), Mark Lathwell, Keith Dutch, Keith Parsons, Richard Johnson, Ian Blackwell, Andy Caddick, Jamie Grove, Pete Trego, Piran Holloway and Julian Wyatt (Second XI Coach).

Front row, left to right – Graham Rose, Mike Burns, Kevin Shine (First XI Coach), Michael Hill (President SCCC), Marcus Trescothick, Rob Turner and Peter Bowler.

SOMERSET

M.E. Trescothick	c Afridi b Ormond	18
P.D. Bowler	b Afridi	42
* J. Cox	b Afridi	44
I.D. Blackwell	b Afridi	15
M. Burns	c Maddy b Wells	21
K.A. Parsons	not out	60
¶ R.J. Turner	not out	37
K.P. Dutch		
R.L. Johnson		
A.R. Caddick		
P.S. Jones		
	19LB 5W	34

TOTAL (5 wickets, 50 overs) 271

1-40, 2-107, 3-132, 4-149, 5-176

Leicestershire Bowling	O	M	R	W	w	nb
J. Ormond	10	2	38	1	2	0
S.A.J. Boswell	2	0	23	0	9	0
P.A.J. DeFreitas	10	1	57	0	2	0
V.J. Wells	10	1	40	1	0	0
D.L. Maddy	8	0	47	0	1	0
A. Afridi	10	0	47	3	1	0

LEICESTERSHIRE

T.R. Ward	b Parsons	54
A. Afridi	c Turner b Johnson	20
D.L. Maddy	c&b Dutch	49
* V.J. Wells	c Turner b Parsons	3
B.F. Smith	c Trescothick b Dutch	15
D.I. Stevens	lbw b Jones	23
¶ N.D. Burns	c Turner b Jones	6
A. Habib	c Dutch b Blackwell	15
P.A.J. DeFreitas	b Johnson	14
J. Ormond	not out	8
S.A.J. Boswell	b Jones	2
	3LB 2W 6NB	11

TOTAL (all out, 45.4 overs) 230

1-20, 2-105, 3-111 4-142, 5-156, 6-171, 7-182, 8-194, 9-225, 10-230

Somerset Bowling	O	M	R	W	w	nb
A.R. Caddick	10	2	33	0	0	2
R.L. Johnson	8	0	39	2	2	0
P.S. Jones	7.4	0	40	3	0	0
K.A. Parsons	6	0	40	2	0	1
K.P. Dutch	10	0	50	2	0	0
I.D. Blackwell	4	0	25	1	0	0

*Captain   ¶Wicketkeeper

Pre-Season 2001 Press Call

Ian Blackwell

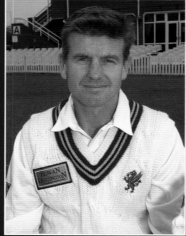

Peter Bowler

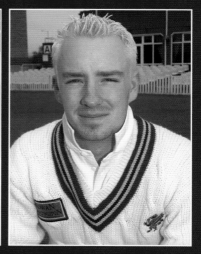

Matt Bulbeck

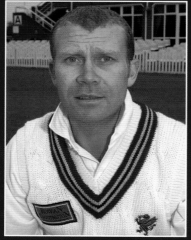

Mike Burns

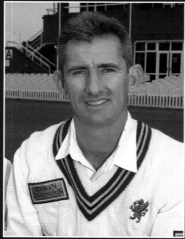

Andy Caddick

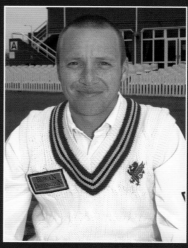

Keith Dutch

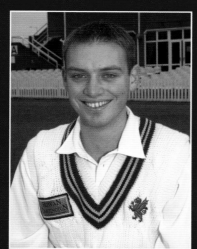

Carl Gazzard

Jamie Grove

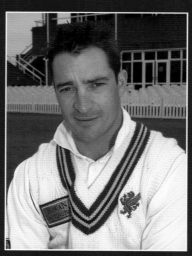

Piran Holloway

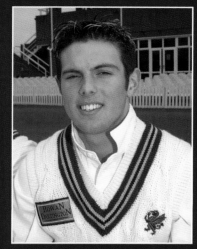

Chris Hunkin

Richard Johnson

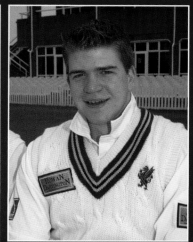

Ian Jones

Stefan Jones

Jason Kerr

Mark Lathwell

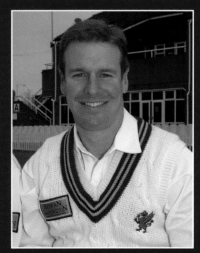

Keith Parsons

Arul Suppiah

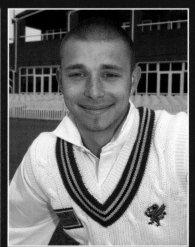

Pete Trego

Rob Turner   Marcus Trescothick   Matt Wood

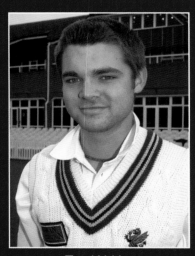

Tom Webley   Joe Tucker

Another boundary for Mike Burns.

Opposite, bottom: 2001 Somerset Squad.
Back row – Matt Wood, Tom Webley, Joe Tucker, Steffan Jones, Jason Kerr, Matt Bulbeck, Ian Jones, Carl Gazzard, Chris Hunkin, Arul Suppiah, Andy Hurry (Fitness Instructor) and Darren Veness (First XI Physio).
Middle row – Mark Lathwell, Keith Dutch, Keith Parsons, Richard Johnson, Ian Blackwell, Andy Caddick, Jamie Grove, Pete Trego, Julian Wyatt (Second XI Coach), Ross Dewar (Second XI Physio) and Piran Holloway.
Front Row – Graham Rose, Mike Burns, Kevin Shine (First XI Coach), Michael Hill (President SCCC), Marcus Trescothick, Rob Turner and Peter Bowler.

Above left: Marcus Trescothick on his way to the man of the match award winning innings against Glamorgan in the fourth round of the Cheltenham & Gloucester Trophy on 11 July 2001. The wicket-keeper for the visitors is Matt Maynard.

After being put into bat the visitors made 269 for six from their 50 overs, of which Maynard contributed an unbeaten 93, while Andy Caddick claimed two for 44 from his 10 overs and Richard Johnson two for 64, also from 10.

Somerset made light work of their response thanks to Trescothick who raced to his 50 off just 23 balls and his century off 69 before being out for 121 which came off 83 balls with 20 fours.

Skipper Jamie Cox then took over and hit an unbeaten 63 off 55 deliveries with two fours and three sixes to see Somerset home by seven wickets with more than eight overs to spare.

Above right: The Somerset players await the arrival of a new Warwickshire batsman in the home semi-final game in the Cheltenham & Gloucester Trophy in 2001.

This match was a real cliff hanger and after seeing the visitors reach 101 without loss they were limited to 228 for eight, thanks to three wickets from Richard Johnson and economic spells from Mike Burns and Keith Parsons.

The Somerset reply started badly with three wickets down for six runs before a recovery was mounted, but even at 130 for six with 19 overs left it looked a tall order.

However Keith Dutch (61 not out) and Rob Turner (42 not out) then came together to add 100 runs in 87 balls to see Somerset through to the Lord's Final.

Jamie Grove centre of picture is performing the twelfth man duties.

Rght: Warwickshire batted first in the C & G semi-final and scored 228 for eight.

Simon Jones

A frustrated Simon Jones can only look on as Peter Bowler makes his way towards 164 for Somerset against Glamorgan at the County Ground in the championship in July 2001. Bowler and Mike Burns at the non strikers end who made 81, added 135 for the fourth wicket.

Ian Blackwell then joined Bowler and proceeded to blast his way to 102 as the pair added 163 together a new fifth wicket partnership for the hosts against Glamorgan out of an eventual total of 600 for eight declared, which helped Somerset win by an innings and 67 runs.

C&G Final v Leicestershire at Lord's 2001

Above: Somerset Captain James Cox holds the C & G Trophy aloft.

Opposite page, top left: Steffan Jones who captured the final wicket. *Top right:* Andy Caddick (left) and Keith Dutch parade the trophy. *Centre:* Somerset give their supporters something to cheer about. *Bottom:* The joyous Somerset cup-winning side.

Some of the Key Players

Andy Caddick

Andy Caddick was Somerset's most successful England bowler seen opposite in action in 2005.

Though born in New Zealand the big man became one of Somerset's favourite sons and between 1993 and 2003 he played in 62 Test matches for England in which he took 234 wickets at an average of 29.91 with a best of seven for 46.

Caddick also played in 54 One Day Internationals in which he took 69 wickets at 28.47.

Caddick made his first class debut in 1991 and between then and 2009 he played in 191 first class matches in which he scored 3139 runs at an average of 17.25 with a best of 92.

The big man bowled 6977.1 first class overs and took 875 wickets at an average of 25.81, with a best of nine for 32 against Lancashire at Taunton in 1993, a game in which Marcus Trescothick made his debut.

Caddick was never happier than when he had the ball in his hand.

Giles Clarke the Somerset Chairman presenting the mounted ball with which Andy Caddick took his 1000th wicket which was against Yorkshire in August 2005.

Mike Burns

Above left: Mike Burns batting at Bath on the opening day of the championship match against Worcestershire in June 2005.

Above right: All rounder Mike Burns, who moved to join Somerset from Warwickshire in 1997 was a more than useful performer with both bat and ball as well as being able to keep wicket.
Here the ever reliable Rob Turner is diving to try to hang on to a chance off Burns.

Left: Mike joined Somerset in 1997 from Warwickshire – a true all rounder he is seen here in one day action in 2004.

Matt Wood

Opening batsman Matt Wood who hailed from Exmouth where he played his club cricket before appearing for Devon made his Somerset debut in 2001. Between then and when he departed for Nottinghamshire the right handed batsman who hit a career best of 297 against Yorkshire at Taunton, played in 69 championship games.

He was also a member of the Somerset side that lifted the T20 Cup in 2005 and the team that beat the Australians at Taunton in a one day match.

Keith Parsons

Parsons made his Somerset debut in 1992 and between then and 2008 he played in 130 first class games for the county in which he scored 5324 runs at an average of 28.62, with a best of 193 not out against West Indies in 2000. He also took 106 first class wickets at 43.83 with a best of five for 13 against Lancashire also in 2000.

Parsons enjoyed huge success in one day cricket playing in 247 List A matches, including the 2001 Cheltenham & Gloucester Trophy winning final, in which he scored 5225 runs at 29.68 with a best of 121 against Worcestershire, while in T20 he played in 29 matches, including the 2005 final winning side, scoring 463 runs at 22.05 with a best of 57 not out and took 18 wickets at 23.89 with a best of three for 12.

Opposite:
Top left: Parsons played many memorable innings in both one day and first class cricket, but sadly not on this occasion.

Top right: Parsons on his way to a match winning innings of 60 not out against Leicestershire in the 2001 Final of the Cheltenham & Gloucester Trophy at Lord's which he followed up by taking three for 40.

Centre left: Parsons was named as the Man of the Match at Lord's and is seen here celebrating after the presentation.

Centre: Parsons appeals for another wicket against Leicestershire at Taunton in 2005.

Centre right middle: Parsons batting against Kent in the Totesport League at Bath and *centre far right* batting against Worcestershire also at The Rec, both in 2005.

Bottom left: Parsons is seen here batting in a pre-season friendly against Gloucestershire at the County Ground. The wicket-keeper is Steve Snell who later played for Somerset before being appointed an Academy Director.

Bottom right: Parsons giving it his all bowling at the County Ground. The umpire is Ian Gould.

Below left: Local hero Keith Parsons became a household name after producing a number of match winning performances in one day cricket for Somerset.

Below right: Keith Parsons the bowler in Totesport League against against Durham in August 2005. Later the all rounder donned the pads to hit a vital unbeaten 44 to see Somerset to victory by five wickets with 22 balls to spare.

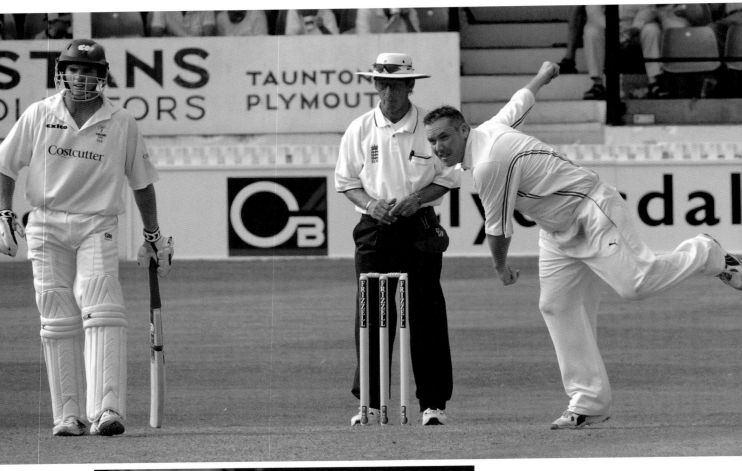

Ian Blackwell

Above: Ian Blackwell the bowler, seen here in action against Yorkshire in 2005. Former Somerset player Jeremy Lloyds is the umpire.

Left: All rounder Ian Blackwell joined Somerset from Derbyshire in 2000 and quickly endeared himself to the County Ground regulars with his big hitting antics and his slow left arm spin bowling.

Ian Blackwell walking back to his mark during the championship match against Leicestershire in July 2005. John Steele is the umpire.

From left to right: Ian Blackwell in determined mood bowling against Durham at the County Ground in July 2005; 'Just how unlucky can a bowler get?' Ian Blackwell's facial expression says it all after he has sent down a delivery to a Durham batsman in July 2005 at the County Ground; Ian Blackwell just cannot believe his bad luck bowling against Durham. The umpire is Roy Palmer, another former Somerset player who went onto the first class umpires list.

Opposite, clockwise from top left:
Blackwell bowling in 2005; at the County Ground in July 2005 ahead of the T20 Finals Day at the Oval; Bowling again, this time the umpire is former Somerset player Roy Palmer; Ian Blackwell in pre season training March 2005, (note the old Supporters Stand in the background).

Right: Blackie the Master Blaster – Big hitting Ian Blackwell quickly established himself as a big hitting all rounder and here he shows just why he was so popular as he heaves another big six over the boundary.

This time it is the Yorkshire bowlers who are being put to the sword as the Somerset left hander helps himself to more runs on his way to 116 in the high scoring Totesport League match which the hosts won by two runs.

Below: Ian Blackwell bowling against Scotland in the Totesport League in June 2005, with former Somerset favourite Graham Burgess the umpire.

Rob Turner

Rob Turner the batsman in action helps another delivery to the boundary.

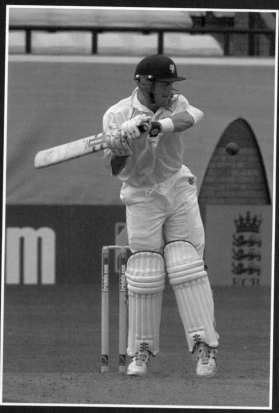

Jamie Cox

Jamie Cox who led Somerset to three One Day Finals during his time at the County Ground, in 1999, 2001 and 2002, is seen here batting against Surrey in the championship in late August 2001.

Cox joined Somerset as captain in 1999 and between then and 2004 when he left the top order right-handed batsman played in 91 first class matches in which he scored 6688 runs at 47.43, including 17 centuries with a best of 250 against Nottinghamshire at Trent Bridge in 2004. He topped 1000 runs in a season four times with his best season being 1999 when he hit 1617.

Cox also played in 110 List A matches in which he scored 3598 runs.

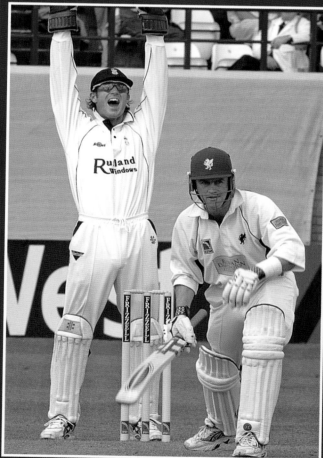

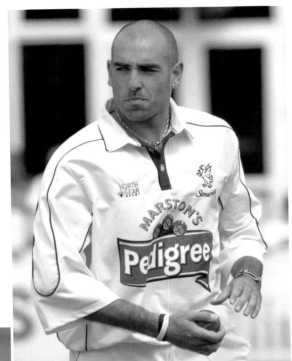

Richard Johnson

Left: Richard Johnson walking back to his mark to prepare to bowl the next ball for Somerset against Durham at the County Ground in July 2005.

Below: That's out! Richard Johnson seems in little doubt about the outcome of this appeal against Lancashire in May 2004 neither does wicket-keeper Rob Turner nor Peter Bowler.

Above left: Richard Johnson in full flight bowling against Warwickshire in the Totesport League at Taunton in September 2005. Above right: Richard Johnson receives the ball on his way back to his mark in the opening Totesport League game of the 2004 season against Derbyshire in April.

Below Richard Johnson moves quickly to his right to field a ball off his own bowling in the Cheltenham & Gloucester Trophy semifinal against Warwickshire on 1 August 2001.

The former Middlesex bowler's three for 42 off his 10 over stint enabled the hosts to limit Warwickshire to 228 for eight from their 50 overs, which Somerset chased down with four wickets and overs to spare. This was another fantastic day's cricket and sent the County Ground fans home buzzing at the prospect of another Lord's Final

2002 — 2004

Clockwise from top left: Piran Holloway opening the batting made 33 in the second innings for Somerset against Surrey in July 2002; Matt Wood clips a delivery to fine leg on his way to making 131 in the championship match against Surrey in July 2002; Simon Francis bowling against Leicestershire in July 2005 — Francis joined Somerset from Hampshire in 2002; Arul Suppiah pictured in 2005. Although primarily a right handed opening batsman Arul was also a very useful left arm spinner which he proved when he set a new T20 world record by taking six wickets for five runs against Glamorgan in Cardiff in 2011.

Opposite: Cornishman Neil Edwards was another young player who came through the Academy at the County Ground.

Above: Fast bowler Simon Francis joined Somerset from Hampshire in 2002 and between then and 2006 he played in 40 first class matches and took 105 wickets at 38.90 with a best of five for 42.

Francis set a new Cheltenham & Gloucester Trophy one day record for Somerset when he took eight for 66 against Derbyshire at Derby on 5 May 2004, a return which completely changed the course of the game enabling the visitors to eventually win by 14 runs.

Left: Peter Bowler batting against Worcestershire in the quarter final of the Cheltenham & Gloucester Trophy competition on 17 July 2002 – Steve Rhodes is the wicket keeper.

Somerset won this game by four wickets. After dismissing Worcestershire for 271 in 49 overs, Steffan Jones taking three for 47, Somerset – despite losing the services of Marcus Trescothick with a broken thumb – reached 273 for six in 47.3 overs, thanks to 121 from Keith Parsons and 47 from Rob Turner.

 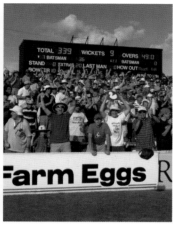 

Above left: Keith Parsons won the Man of the Match Award after he hit a match-winning 121 off 100 balls to help Somerset beat Worcestershire in the quarter-final of the Cheltenham & Gloucester Trophy at the County Ground by four wickets.

The match was played in front of a full house on a beautiful sunny day. After Worcestershire made 271, the hosts slipped to 36 for two before Parsons pulled the game round, assisted by Mike Burns (24), Ian Blackwell (30) and Rob Turner (47) with whom he added 106 for the fifth wicket in 20 overs before victory was achieved by four wickets with 15 balls to spare.

Steven Rhodes is the Worcestershire wicket-keeper.

Above centre: Somerset fans savouring every last minute of the team's remarkable victory over Kent in the semi-final of the Cheltenham & Gloucester Trophy 2002.

Above right: Steffan Jones runs the gauntlet of jubilant Somerset fans after he has taken two for 51 to help the hosts beat Kent in the semi final of the Cheltenham & Gloucester Trophy 2002.

Below: A delighted Keith Parsons sprints off the field after helping to bowl his side to victory over Kent in the semi final of the Cheltenham & Gloucester Trophy with four for 55 from his eight overs.

There's people on the pitch – it's all over! Somerset beat Kent by five runs in the semi-final of the Cheltenham & Gloucester Trophy in August 2002 in front of a packed house to reach their second Lord's final in as many seasons.

Opposite, top: Somerset on pre season press day 28 March 2003 – walking over to take their seats for the squad photograph.

Opposite, bottom: Somerset squad in 2003.
Back row, left to right – Andy Hurry (Fitness Instructor), Ross Dewar (assistant physiotherapist), Arul Suppiah, Wes Durston, Neil Edwards, Ian Blackwell, Matt Wood, Darren Veness (Head of injury prevention) and Mark Garaway (Second XI Coach).
Second row, left to right – Kevin Shine (First XI Coach), Piran Holloway, James Bryant, Steffan Jones, Simon Francis, Carl Gazzard, Aaron Laraman, Matt Bulbeck, Keith Dutch and Gerry Stickley (First Team Scorer).
Front row, left to right – Peter Bowler, Rob Turner, Marcus Trescothick, Michael Hill (President SCCC), Mike Burns (Captain), Giles Clarke (Chairman SCCC), Andy Caddick, Richard Johnson and Keith Parsons.

Clockwise from top left: Mike Burns and Andy Caddick enjoy a lighter moment on Press Day 2003; James Hildreth on his way to scoring 51 to help Somerset beat Worcestershire in the T20 Cup in July 2004; West Indian Test bowler Nixon McLean joined Somerset from Hampshire in 2003 and played at the County Ground until 2005 during which time he played in 33 first class matches and took 120 wickets at an average of 29.22, with a best of six for 79; West Indian Test bowler Nixon McLean seen here bowling against Derbyshire in the opening Totesport League match in April 2004, in which he claimed three for 21 from his six overs.

Above left: Australian batsman Ricky Ponting played a handful of matches for Somerset in 2004 and proved to be another popular overseas player during his short stay, playing in three championship matches scoring 297 runs with an average of 99. He also appeared in four Totesport League games, scoring 298 runs at an average of 99.33.

Above right: A classic Keith Parsons shot bringing him another boundary to see him to 51 batting against Derbyshire in the Norwich Union National League in April 2004. Former Somerset player Luke Sutton is the Derbyshire 'keeper. Somerset won the match by 109 runs.

2005
More Glory

Somerset 2005 in their T20 kit.
Back row, left to right – Darren Veness, head of injury prevention, Matt Wood, Carl Gazzard, Mike Parsons, Arul Suppiah, Mark Garaway (First Team Coach).
Middle row, left to right – Brian Rose (Director of Cricket), Aaron Laraman, Neil Edwards, Andy Caddick, Rob Turner, Richard Johnson and Mike Burns.
Front row, left to right – Simon Francis, Wes Durston, Gareth Andrew, Graeme Smith, Ian Blackwell, Keith Parsons and Charl Langeveldt.

Graeme Smith

Graeme Smith had a huge influence on Somerset in the few short months he spent at the County Ground during the summer of 2005, in which time the Club recorded a historic one day victory over the mighty Australians and then the South African captain led the team to their first ever T20 Cup success.

The twenty-three-year old Smith arrived in time to make his championship debut against Leicestershire at Oakham School at the start of June where he was greeted by a washed out first day in a game that was drawn.

Next Smith was off to Bath where against Worcestershire he added 88 for the third wicket with Sanath Jayasuriya before he was out for 55.

The following week Smith led Somerset to victory over reigning world champions Australia in a 50 over match that was played in front of a packed house at the County Ground.

Chasing 343 for victory Smith opened the innings and scored 108 sharing in an opening partnership with Sanath Jayasuriya who made 101, to pave the way for some of Somerset's youngsters to complete a memorable win.

In the return match against Leicestershire at the County Ground the left hander hit 311 which included 27 fours and 11 sixes to lead his side to victory by 10 wickets.

Smith made his biggest impact in the Twenty20 Cup competition which was first introduced into the English domestic season in 2003.

Under Smith's inspirational leadership Somerset qualified for the quarter finals of the T20 Cup for the first time where they travelled to Northamptonshire and won by four wickets to book their place at final's day at the Oval.

In the semi final Somerset beat Leicestershire by four runs to earn the right to face hot favourites Lancashire in the rain-delayed final that was reduced to 16 overs per side.

Chasing down 115 for victory Smith opened the innings and remained unbeaten on 64 as Somerset reached 118 for three in 14.1 overs.

Smith was an inspirational captain and leader and flew back to South Africa the day after the final leaving so much for him to be remembered by.

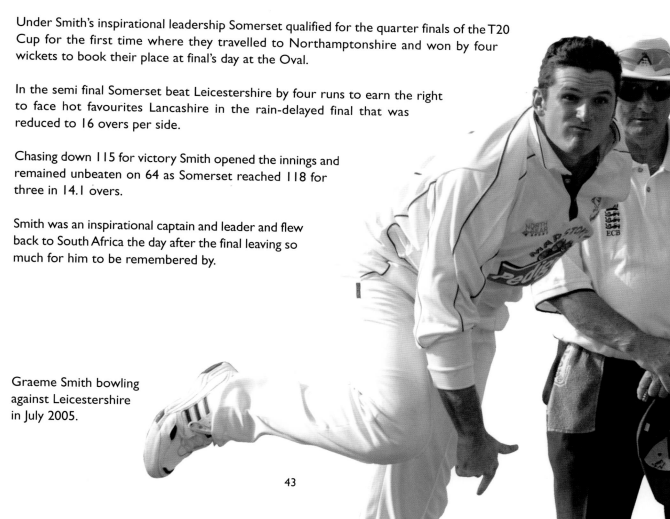

Graeme Smith bowling against Leicestershire in July 2005.

Opposite, top left:
Graeme Smith batting
against Worcestershire at
Bath in June 2005.

Top right: Graeme Smith
batting for Somerset
against Worcestershire
at Taunton in June 2005.

Bottom three:
Graeme Smith batting
for Somerset against
Worcestershire at Bath
in June 2005. Smith was
a great timer of the ball
but also a very powerful
batsman.

Above right: Graeme Smith
on his way to a match-
winning 108 against
Australia in June 2005.

Right: Graham Smith the
bowler against Kent in the
Totesport League in June
2005 at The Rec in Bath.

More action from
Graeme Smith batting
at Bath against
Worcestershire.

Above: Charl Langeveldt (left) pictured with Graeme Smith.

Left: Graeme Smith batting against Kent at Bath in 2005.

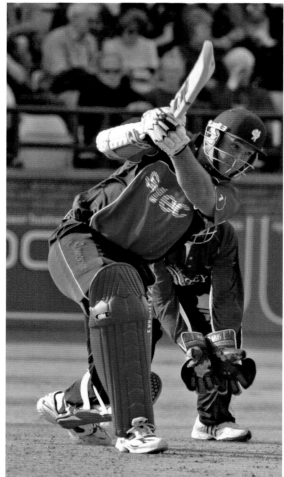

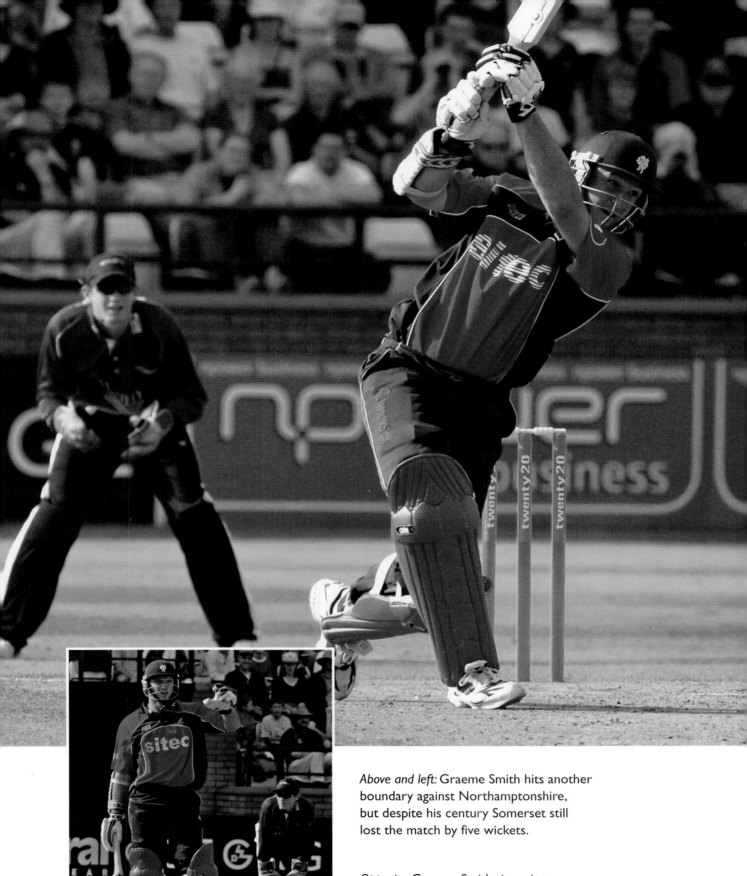

Above and left: Graeme Smith hits another boundary against Northamptonshire, but despite his century Somerset still lost the match by five wickets.

Opposite: Graeme Smith times it to perfection on his way to a century in the Northamptonshire game. Matt Wood is at the non-strikers end and Riki Wessels is the 'keeper.

Top: Graeme Smith looks out across the County Ground in a rare quiet moment during his all too brief stay with Somerset

Above left: Hang onto this for me skipper – Graeme Smith, who proved to be an inspirational captain during his short stay is seen here undertaking some of his duties during the championship match with Leicestershire, in which he scored 311.

Above right: South African captain Graeme Smith batting at Bath.

Opposite: Graeme Smith batting for Somerset against Worcestershire at Bath in June 2005.

Above: Graeme Smith batting against Worcestershire at Bath.

Left and opposite: Graeme Smith bowling against Leicestershire in July 2005, with former Somerset favourite Merv Kitchen doing the umpiring duties.

Graeme Smith on his way to scoring 105 for Somerset against Northamptonshire in the T20 Cup competition at Taunton on 3 July 2005. The bowler looking on is Ben Phillips who later joined Somerset and who eventually caught Smith to dismiss him.

John Francis (left) and Graeme Smith going out to open the Somerset innings on day one of the championship match against Worcestershire at Bath on 8 June 2005.

Above: Graeme Smith batting at Bath.

Below left: Sanath Jayasuriya taking a quick run against Worcestershire at Bath in June 2005.
Below right: James Hildreth on his way to scoring 86 against Durham in July 2005.

Above: Simon Francis celebrates having Sussex batsman Mike Yardy caught by wicket-keeper Rob Turner in the Totesport League on 30 May 2005.

Left: Caddick goes up for a confident appeal against Leicestershire's Darren Maddy in the championship match at the County Ground in July 2005. Somerset captain Graeme Smith, who had scored 311 out of Somerset's first innings total of 566 and is fielding at first slip, joins in.

Opposite: Andy Caddick in a classic action pose bowling against Leicestershire in the championship on 8 July 2005.

Left: All rounder Wes Durston played in every round of the T20 Cup-winning team of 2005 and in July that year is seen here fielding in the championship match against Leicestershire.

Below left: All rounder Wes Durston in pre-season training during March 2005 ahead of what was to turn out to be a highly successful season.

Below right: Wes Durston bowling against Leicestershire in July 2005.

Above: Matt Wood consigns another delivery to the boundary on his way to making 54 against Northamptonshire in the T20 in 2005.
Below: Action from the opening day of Somerset's championship match against Yorkshire in Taunton on 10 August 2005.

Above: Local boy Mike Parsons was another one of Somerset's youngsters who played in the memorable victory over Australia in June 2005.

Opposite, top left: Matt Wood on his way to a List A best score of 129 against Yorkshire in August 2005.

Top right: Simon Francis bowling against Kent in the Totesport League match at Bath in June 2005. Rob Key is the batsman at the non-strikers end.

Centre left: Matt Wood on his way to scoring 39 to help Somerset to a 95 run victory over Gloucestershire in the T20 Cup in July 2005. The 'keeper is Steve Adshead.

Centre right: John Francis batting in the same match.

Bottom left and right: Keith Parsons bowling with Graeme Smith in close attendance against Kent in the Totesport League at Bath in June 2005. Rob Key is the Kent batsman.

Left: Wes Durston making an unbeaten 13 against Gloucestershire in the T20 Cup in July 2005.

Below left: Somerset beat Leicestershire by 10 wickets in July 2005, in a game that featured 311 from Graeme Smith, which included 24 fours and 11 sixes. Here the Somerset captain is fielding at first slip next to 'keeper Carl Gazzard.

Below right: A very happy Arul Suppiah at the County Ground in August 2005.

Opposite: Skipper Graeme Smith and Mike Burns have a mid wicket conference whilst batting together at Bath against Worcesetershire in 2005.

Left: Gareth Andrew decides to let a delivery from a Derbyshire bowler go by watched by former Somerset player Luke Sutton in September 2005.

Below: More action from the Totesport League match against Scotland at the County Ground in August 2005. South African born Jonathan Beukes is seen here on his way to scoring 92 before being bowled by Ian Blackwell, watched by 'keeper Carl Gazzard.

Marcus Trescothick was centrally contracted to England for a number of seasons and was only occasionally available to Somerset. Here the left handed opener is seen playing against Surrey on 2 May when he made 52 in his only Totesport League appearance of the 2005 season.

Above: First XI Coach Mark Garaway (centre) carries out the 12th man duties during a break in the championship match against Leicestershire on 7 July 2005.

Pictured left to right are – John Steele (umpire), Ian Blackwell, Mike Burns, Matt Wood, John Francis, Graeme Smith (behind), Andy Caddick, Carl Gazzard, Keith Parsons and Simon Francis. Hidden out of view in picture are James Hildreth and Wes Durston.

Opposite, clockwise from top left: Big hitting Ian Blackwell blasted his way to 45 in next to no time to help Somerset beat their old rivals Gloucestershire in the T20 in July 2005; Wes Durston batting against Gloucestershire in the T20 Cup in July 2005; Ian Blackwell blasts another one to the boundary against Warwickshire in the Totesport League match on 5 September 2005, a game which Somerset won by four wickets. Nick Knight is fielding at slip and the 'keeper is Tony Frost.

Right: Matt Wood hits one skywards against Northamptonshire in the T20 and hopes it doesn't fall to hand.

Above: Rob Woodman in action during his debut against Durham in the Totesport League in 2005.

Opposite, top: Rob Woodman walking back to his mark in the Totesport League game against Durham at Taunton in August 2005.

Within days of signing his first full-time contract in 2005 Rob Woodman, a local all rounder who graduated through the Somerset Academy made his debut in the Totesport 40 over League match against Durham at the County Ground.

Opposite, bottom: Rob Woodman listens to the advice of his captain Ian Blackwell on his debut.

Above left: Local boy Mike Parsons played in a handful of matches for Somerset and in June 2005 he was part of the victorious side that beat Australia at Taunton in a 50 over game.

Here he is seen bowling against Lancashire in the championship at the County Ground in May 2005.

Above right: Matt Wood batting in a pre-season match at Taunton in April 2005. The Devonian enjoyed a successful year in 2005 during which he recorded his career-best score of 297 against Yorkshire at Taunton.

Right: Big hitting Ian Blackwell blasting his way to 114 in the Totesport League against Yorkshire in August 2005.

Opposite: Arul Suppiah looks anxiously as his leg glance goes just wide of Yorkshire 'keeeper Ismail Dawood at the County Ground, Taunton in August 2005.

Sri Lankan batsman Sanath Jayasuriya spent the first part of the 2005 summer playing for Somerset. Here he demonstrates one of his array of attacking shots, all played with exquisite timing against Worcestershire at Bath on a rare sunny day.

Above: Graeme Smith (left) and Sanath Jayasuriya shared a third wicket partnership of 88 on the opening day of the championship match between Somerset and Worcestershire on 8 June 2005 at The Rec in Bath.

Below: Sanath Jayasuriaya goes on the attack for Somerset against Worcestershire at Bath in June 2005.

Above: Two of the young brigade – all rounder Gareth Andrew from Bruton and Taunton boy Mike Parsons, who were both in the Somerset side that beat the Aussies on that never to be forgotten day on 15 June 2005.

Opposite, top left: Sri Lankan Test player Sanath Jayasuriya spent the first part of the 2005 season with Somerset. Here he is seen bowling in the Totesport League against Scotland on 17 June – a game the visitors won by 15 runs.

Top right: Umpire Graham Burgess, a former Somerset player, has to take avoiding action after the ball is driven straight back at him.

Bottom left: Sanath Jayasuriya seen here on his way to 73 in the championship match against Lancashire at the County Ground in May 2005.

Bottom right: Sanath Jayasuriaya batting against Worcestershire at Bath.

Right: Sanath Jayasuriya had moved onto 32 when he edged Darren Maddy to first slip where Hylton Ackerman took the catch watched by Leciestershire 'keeper Paul Nixon in the Totesport League on 1 May 2005.

Below: Sanath Jayasuriya on his way to making 32 in the Totesport League match against Leicestershire on 1 May 2005 which the hosts won by eight wickets.

Charl Langeveldt bowling for Somerset in their Totesport League match against Durham in August 2005 at Taunton. The hosts won the match by five wickets, thanks to 76 from Matt Wood and an unbeaten 44 from Keith Parsons. Earlier Durham had been restricted to 222 for seven, Langeveldt and Wes Durston taking two wickets each.

During his stay at the County Ground the South African fast bowler played in six championship matches in which he claimed 15 wickets, seven Totesport League matches in which he took seven wickets and three T20 matches including the final at the Oval against Lancashire.

Above left and right: Charl Langeveldt seen here bowling against Leicestershire in July 2005 in the championship match, which Somerset won by 10 wickets. Graeme Smith scored 311 in this match, his fellow countryman Langeveldt claimed three wickets in each innings.

Left: Charl Langevedlt giving it his all bowling for Somerset against Leicestershire at Taunton in 2005. Langeveldt later had a spell with Kent.

Opposite: Charl Langeveldt in full flow bowling against Leicestershire at Taunton in July 2005 a game in which he took three wickets in each innings, sharing the opening duties with Andy Caddick.

The Day We Beat Australia – 15 June 2005

Graeme Smith bowled seven overs and took one for 61 as Australia scored 342 for five from their 50 overs, which they expected to be enough to see them to victory.

However the young South African skipper then buckled on his pads and shared an opening partnership of 197 with Sanath Jayasuriya in just 23 overs of which he made 108 and his Sri Lankan partner 101.

Afterwards the Australians reined the game back in somewhat and reduced the hosts to 291 for six before Carl Gazzard the twenty-three-year-old 'keeper and twenty-year-old James Hildreth came together to see the hosts home with an unbroken partnership of 54 with 19 balls to spare.

This game goes down in Somerset history as one of the greatest one day victories ever seen at the County Ground and will live in the memory of those who were there.

Somerset v Australia

One-day Friendly
At Taunton on 15th June, 2005
Umpires: G. Sharp & J.F Steele

Australia won the toss and elected to bat
Somerset won by 4 wickets
Scorers: G.A. Stickley & P Lane

AUSTRALIA

M.L. Hayden	retired out	76
S.M. Katich	c Hildreth b S. Francis	12
* R.T. Ponting	retired out	80
D.R. Martyn	st Gazzard b Smith	44
M.J. Clarke	not out	63
M.E.K. Hussey	b Jayasuriya	51
+ B. Haddin	not out	5
S.R. Watson		
B. Lee		
M.S. Kasprowicz		
G.D. McGrath		
	2LB 9W	11

TOTAL (for 5 wickets, 50 overs) 342

1-60, 2-101 3-211 4-221 5-320

Somerset Bowling	O	M	R	W	w	nb
Andrew	5.2	0	52	0	0	0
S. Francis	8.0	0	56	1	1	0
M. Parsons	8.0	0	57	0	0	0
S.T. Jayasuriya	8.0	0	47	1	3	0
Smith	7.0	0	61	1	3	0
K. Parsons	7.4	0	43	0	0	0
Blackwell	6.0	0	24	0	0	0

SOMERSET

* G.C. Smith	st Haddin b Clarke	108
S.T. Jayasuriya	c Hussey b McGrath	101
J.D. Francis	b McGrath	23
I.D. Blackwell	b Watson	25
K.A. Parsons	lbw b Hussey	1
M.J. Wood	c Clarke b Hussey	17
J.C. Hildreth	not out	38
+ C.M. Gazzard	not out	21
G.M. Andrew		
S.R.G. Francis		
M. Parsons		
	5LB 2W 4NB	11

TOTAL (For 6 wkts, 46.5 overs) 345

1-197 2-231 3-254, 4-258, 5-277, 6-291

Australia Bowling	O	M	R	W	w	nb
Lee	4.0	0	26	0	0	0
McGrath	10.0	0	49	2	1	1
Kasprowicz	8.0	0	89	0	0	3
Watson	8.5	0	72	1	1	0
Clarke	10.0	0	63	1	0	0
Hussey	6.0	0	41	2	0	0

*Captain   +Wicketkeeper

Above: Somerset mascot for the day Charlie Tudball, pictured with Graeme Smith ahead of the historic one day victory over Australia at the County Ground on 15 June 2005.

Below: Somerset captain Graeme Smith and Ricky Ponting the captain of Australia toss the coin ahead of the one day match at the County Ground. The tourists won the toss and chose to bat first.

Above: Mascot for the day Charlie Tudball, pictured with Mike Burns and Australian captain Ricky Ponting ahead of Somerset's memorable one day victory on 15 June 2005.

Below: Mike Burns and Ricky Ponting shake hands before the one day match between Somerset and Australia on 15 June 2005.

Top left: James Hildreth who hit a vital 38 not out in the Somerset victory over Australia in June 2005.
Top right: Action from the Somerset against Australia game – Sanath Jayasuriya is the bowler.
Above: Michael Clarke on his way to an unbeaten 63 watched by Carl Gazzard on 15 June 2005.

Keith Parsons bowling against Australia during the one day match on June 15th 2005.
The batsman at the non-striker's end is Ricky Ponting and the umpire is George Sharp.

A packed crowd at the County Ground enjoying the match.

Ricky Ponting batting for Australia at the County Ground on 15 June 2005, the wicket-keeper is Carl Gazzard.

Left and opposite: Australian captain Ricky Ponting on his way to scoring 80 before he retired.

Carl Gazzard can only look on as the Australian skipper hits another delivery to the boundary.

Ponting played three championship games for Somerset in 2004 and in his four innings scored 297 runs, which included two centuries to end with an average of 99.

Above: Ian Blackwell walks back to his mark before bowling during the 50 over game against Australia on 15 June 2005.

Opposite, top left: Somerset v Australia at the County Ground 15 June 2005, one of the greatest days in recent years when the county beat the mighty tourists in a 50 over game in front of a packed house. Mascot for the day Charlie Tudball from Minehead helps Wes Durston with the twelfth man duties.

Top right: Bruton born Gareth Andrew was one of the Somerset young guns who were members of the team that beat the mighty Australians, captained by Ricky Ponting on that never to be forgotten June day in 2005.

Here the right arm bowler who opened the attack against Matthew Hayden and Simon Katich is running in from the River End past umpire George Sharp.

Centre: Matt Wood enjoys encouragement from the packed house at the County Ground on 15 June 2005 against Australia – little did they know what was to come later in the day.

Bottom left: Keith Parsons bowling to Matt Hayden in the one day game against Australia on 15 June 2005. The 'keeper is Carl Gazzard.

Bottom right: Graeme Smith bowling against Australia watched by umpire George Sharp and the opposing skipper Ricky Ponting.

Above: Australian captain Ricky Ponting on his way to making 80 in the 50 over match at the County Ground on 15 June 2005, watched by wicket-keeper Carl Gazzard.

Left: Gareth Andrew bowling against Australia in June 2005.

Opposite: The crowd gets right behind their Somerset heroes at the County Ground on 15 June 2005 and cheer them to victory over the mighty Australians who were the world champions at the time.

Above: John Francis on his way to scoring 23 in the 50 over match against Australia.

Left and opposite: Graeme Smith on his way to a match-winning 108.

Opposite, top and right: Sanath Jayasuriya made 101 opening the innings with Graeme Smith against Australia adding 197 with his captain to put Somerset well on their way to victory.

Bottom: Sanath Jayasuriya batting against Australia on 15 June.

Right: Sanath Jayasuriya celebrates his century against Australia.

Below: Graeme Smith celebrates his century against Australia.

Left: Graeme Smith batting against Australia.

Below: Sanath Jayasuriya batting against Australia.

Above: Australia's Glenn
McGrath walking back to bowl
at the County Ground.

Right: Australian wicket-keeper
Brad Haddin shares a lighter
moment with Sanath Jayasuriya.

Twenty20 Cup Glory

SOMERSET ENJOYED success for the first time in 2005 in the recently introduced Twenty 20 Cup when they beat the highly fancied Lancashire on a rainy night at the Oval on 30 July.

The road to the final was far from easy and began with a tied game at Cardiff which they lost by the fact that they had lost more wickets – a rule that has since been changed.

Next day they returned to Taunton to beat Worcestershire by 15 runs, thanks to 94 from Matt Wood and some tight bowling by James Hildreth.

The Wurzels were on hand to provide the entertainment before Somerset gained their revenge with a home victory over Glamorgan.

The away match against Northamptonshire at Wantage Road was reduced to 12 overs a side with the hosts being restricted to 95 for 6 before Keith Parsons saw his side home with a boundary off the penultimate ball of the contest.

The game at Bristol against Gloucestershire was abandoned because of rain with Somerset on 61 for seven off 13 overs.

Somerset lost to Northamptonshire in the return game at Taunton despite a fine century from inspirational captain Graeme Smith and they suffered a further defeat when they travelled to play at Edgbaston where in reply to Warwickshire's 172 for eight they were all out for 125.

To qualify for the quarter-finals Somerset needed to beat Gloucestershire at Taunton in the final group match, which they duly achieved. In front of a capacity home crowd Somerset scored 228 for five and then bowled their old rivals out for 133, thanks to Gareth Andrew who took four for 22 and Keith Parsons who claimed three for 12.

In the quarter-finals Somerset returned to face Northamptonshire at Wantage Road where the hosts scored 154 for eight. The visitors achieved their target courtesy of a Keith Parsons boundary off the penultimate ball and 58 from Matt Wood earlier in the innings.

Somerset played Leicestershire, the reigning champions, in the second semifinal at the Oval. Batting first Somerset were struggling at 124 for six before Wes Durston (18) and Carl Gazzard (23) helped them to reach 157.

In reply Leicestershire looked to be cruising at 90 for two in the 12th over before they slipped to 124 for six and eventually ended four runs short to give Somerset a place in the final.

Rain fell heavily after Somerset's game and the final against a star studded Lancashire didn't get underway until 8.15pm as a 16 overs a side match.

Lancahire were restricted to 114 for eight, Richard Johnson taking three for 22 and Andy Caddick two for 21.

When it was Somerset's turn to bat skipper Graeme Smith seemed intent on just one thing and that was leading his side from the front to victory. Smith opened the innings and remained unbeaten on 64 as Somerset reached 118 for three in 14.1 overs.

James Hildreth hit the winning runs to see his side to another memorable victory, just as he had earlier in the year when Somerset beat Australia.

In the semifinal at the Oval on Finals Day, Somerset faced Leicestershire who were the 2004 champions.

Graeme Smith's men posted 157 in reply to which Leicestershire were restricted to 153.

The pictures on the next few pages are all from either the semifinal or the final against Lancashire who Somerset beat to lift the 2005 T20 Trophy for the first time ever.

Above and opposite: Somerset in batting action chasing down the Lancashire target.

Below: Keith Parsons bowling against Leicestershire.

Top and bottom left: Richard Johnson bowling on Finals Day. In both the semifinal and the final the former Middlesex paceman captured three wickets.

Below: Carl Gazzard during his innings of 26 against Leicestershire in the semifinal.

Opposite: Somerset players show their joy at beating Leicestershire in the semifinal.
Top: Marcus Trescothick.
Bottom: Carl Gazzard (Man of the Match) and Richard Johnson.

The mascot race has become a popular feature on T20 Finals Day.

Opposite: The Somerset supporters enjoyed their first taste of a T20 Finals Day – even a shower of rain couldn't dampen their spirits.

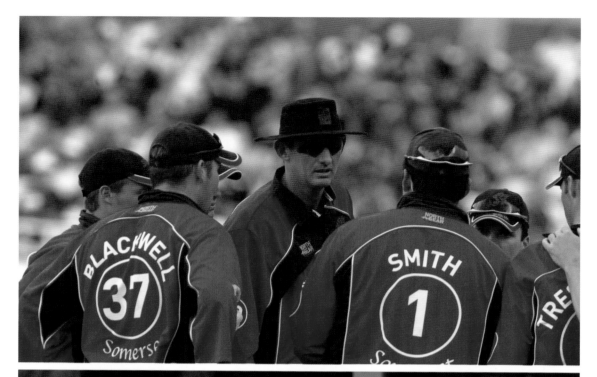

Top: Andy Caddick (in sunglasses) offers some advice to Graeme Smith.

Above: James Hildrith (left) and Ian Blackwell discuss tactics.

Opposite: Action from the semifinal match against Leicestershire.

Above: Somerset celebrate taking a wicket in the final.

Below: Somerset lift the T20 Trophy after beating Lancashire in the final.

Opposite: Skipper Graeme Smith talking to the television after lifting the trophy.

We won the Cup! The taste of success is very sweet for the Somerset players.

Lancashire v Somerset
FINAL

At The Brit Oval on 30th July, 2005
Somerset won by 7 wickets
Umpires: I.J. Gould & P. Willey (3rd J.W. Holder)
Scorers: A. West & G.A. Stickley

Lancashire won the toss
and elected to bat

LANCASHIRE

M.B. Loye	c Johnson b Caddick	5
S.G. Law	run out (Gazzard)	59
A. Flintoff	c Blackwell b Caddick	2
A. Symonds	run out (Durston)	12
D.G. Cork	c Trescothick b Johnson	1
G. Chapple	b Johnson	0
* M.J. Chilton	b Blackwell	9
A.R. Crook	c Gazzard b Johnson	15
+ W.K. Hegg	not out	6
J.M. Anderson		
G. Keedy		
	2LB 3W	5

TOTAL (for 8 wickets, 16 overs) 114

1-6, 2-15, 3-40, 4-41, 5-41, 6-69, 7-101, 8-114

Somerset Bowling	O	M	R	W	w	nb
Caddick	4.0	0	21	2	0	0
Langeveldt	3.0	0	28	0	1	0
Johnson	3.0	0	26	3	1	0
Parsons	3.0	0	13	0	1	0
Blackwell	3.0	0	24	1	0	0

SOMERSET

* G.C. Smith	not out	64
M.E. Trescothick	c Hegg b Flintoff	10
M.J. Wood	b Flintoff	22
I.D. Blackwell	c Law b Keedy	3
J.C. Hildreth	not out	16
K.A. Parsons		
W.J. Durston		
+ C.M. Gazzard		
R.L. Johnson		
C.K. Langeveldt		
A.R. Caddick		
	1LB 2W	3

TOTAL (for 3 wickets, 14.1 overs) 118

1-28, 2-60, 3-65

Lancashire Bowling	O	M	R	W	w	nb
Cork	2.0	0	12	0	0	0
Anderson	1.1	0	14	0	0	0
Flintoff	4.0	0	33	2	1	0
Chapple	2.0	0	23	0	1	0
Keedy	3.0	0	21	1	0	0
Symonds	2.0	0	14	0	0	0

*Captain   +Wicketkeeper

Open top bus ride

The crowds turned out in force to cheer Somerset on their open top bus ride through Taunton.

Ian Blackwell back at the County Ground holding the T20 Trophy with Charlie Tudball lending a hand.

Opposite: Scenes from the open top bus ride.

Somerset players on the open top bus ride. From left to right: Wes Durston, Simon Francis, John Francis, Charl Langeveldt and Ian Blackwell holding the T20 Trophy.

2006 – 2007

Australian left hander Justin Langer arrived in Taunton for a short stay in 2006 but what an impact he had on Somerset.

In his first T20 match Langer teamed up with his fellow Australian Cameron White to help the county score a new world record 250 for three against Gloucestershire in front of a delighted County Ground crowd. During the course of his innings of 90 he added 186 for the second wicket with White, which was a record at that time.

In the eight T20 matches that he played for Somerset that year Langer amassed 464 runs at an average of 66.29, which included four scores over 50.

And that wasn't all because the Aussie Test Match player also appeared in two LV=Championship matches for Somerset, in the second of which, against Surrey at Guildford, he scored 342, a new county record for the highest individual innings.

Langer topped the Somerset championship averages that year with 390 runs from his three innings at an average of 130.

He stay was short and very sweet but it paved the way for him to return to lead Somerset the following season.

Langer batting in the T20 against Gloucestershire in June 2006.

Above left: A determined Justin Langer during his first T20 innings for Somerset against Gloucestershire when he made 90.

Above right: Langer on his way to 97 against Northamptonshire in the T20 at the County Ground on 5 July 2006. The wicket-keeper is Riki Wessels.

Cameron White arrived at the County Ground as a virtual unknown outside his native Australia where he had captained Victoria at the age of twenty.

However he quickly won over the hearts of Somerset supporters when he notched up 172 against Gloucestershire at Bristol in his first match for the county.

That was just the start of a very successful season in which the blond-haired laid-back twenty-two-year-old right-handed batsman and leg break bowler took over the captaincy in May when Ian Blackwell was injured.

That season he played in 12 championship matches in which he scored 1190 runs at an average of 59.50, which included five centuries and a best of 260 not out at Derby.

In the T20 he blitzed his way to 403 runs at an average of 67.17, which included 116 against Gloucestershire to set a new world record best which he then eclipsed with an unbeaten 141 at Worcestershire – where he ended on the losing side. White also scored 323 runs at 46.14 in the Cheltenham & Gloucester Trophy 50 over competition.

The young all rounder returned for the first part of 2007 when he played his part in helping Somerset win promotion back to Division One in the championship.

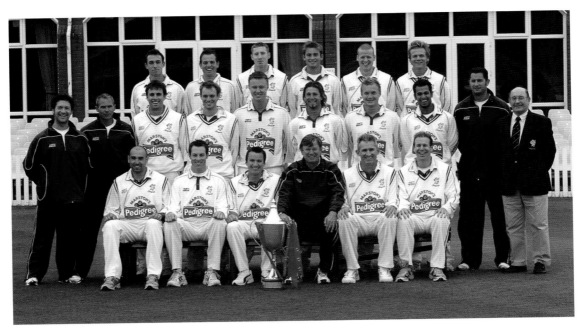

2006 Somerset Squad.
Back row: John Francis, Wes Durston, Sam Spurway, Rob Woodman, Mike Parsons and James Hildreth.
Middle row: Darren Veness (Head of Injury Prevention), Andy Hurry (Fitness Instructor),
Simon Francis, Carl Gazzard, Neil Edwards, Pete Trego, Gareth Andrew, Arul Suppiah,
Jason Kerr (Second XI Coach) and Gerry Stickley (scorer).
Front row: Richard Johnson, Marcus Trescothick, Matt Wood, Brian Rose, Andy Caddick,
and Keith Parsons.

2007 Somerset Squad.
Back row: James Fraser, Rob Woodman, Wes Durston, Craig Kieswetter, Gareth Andrew, Sam
Spurway, Mark Turner and Michael Munday.
Middle row: Jason Kerr (Second XI Coach), Andy Hurry (First XI Coach), James Hildreth, Arul
Suppiah, Carl Gazzard, Steffan Jones, Ben Phillips, Neil Edwards, Pete Sanderson (Assistant Coach
Fielding and Analyst), Darren Veness (Head of Injury Prevention) and Gerry Stickley (Scorer).
Front row: Matt Wood, Ian Blackwell, Marcus Trescothick, Andy Caddick, Brian Rose (Director of
Cricket), Giles Clarke (Chairman SCCC), Roy Kerslake (President SCCC), Justin Langer, Pete Trego,
John Francis and Keith Parsons.

Pre-Season 2007 Press Call

Gareth Andrew

Ian Blackwell

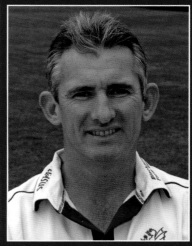

Andy Caddick

Wes Durston

Neil Edwards

John Francis

Carl Gazzard

James Hildreth

Steffan Jones

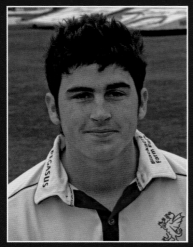

Craig Kieswetter

Michael Munday

Keith Parsons

Ben Phillips

Sam Spurway

Arul Suppiah

Pete Trego

Marcus trescothick

Mark Turner

Matt Wood

Robert Woodman

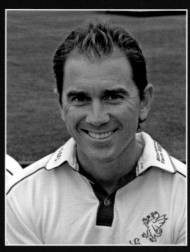

Justin Langer

Jimmy Cook

South African batsman Jimmy Cook who scored 7604 runs for Somerset between 1989 and 1991 at an average of 72.41, with 28 centuries returned to the Club in a coaching capacity for several seasons during Brian Rose's time in charge.

Cook was a classy top order batsman and a prolific run scorer for the county. He topped 2000 runs in each of the seasons he was at Taunton, his best being 2755 in 1991. The previous season he had scored an unbeaten 313 against Glamorgan in Cardiff.

Not only did Cook work with the senior players he also spent a lot of time with the age group teams and worked with several players who went onto play for Somerset at a senior level in years to come.

The Somerset support team who played such an important part in helping the squad win promotion back to the top flight of the championship in 2007.

Left to right – Head Coach Andy Hurry, Darren Veness, Head of Injury Prevention, Jason Kerr, Second XI Coach and Academy Director, Pete Sanderson, Assistant Coach (Fielding) and Analyst.

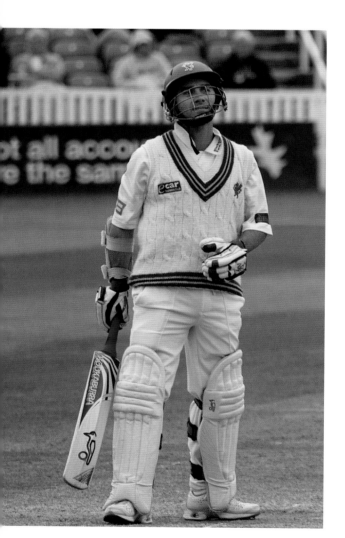

Justin Langer returned to captain Somerset in 2007 and working alongside Director of Cricket Brian Rose and Head Coach Andy Hurry laid the foundations for the Club's most successful period in recent history.

In his first season in charge Langer who played in 104 Test Matches brought that Aussie grit to the Somerset dressing room. He led from the front and set the highest of standards all round, which he expected his team to follow.

In his opening match of the 2007 season against Middlesex at Taunton the left hander scored his second triple century for the Club in as many matches, following on from his record breaking 342 against Surrey in his previous match in 2006.

Langer scored 1231 runs in 2007 and led Somerset to 10 wins and the Division Two championship and a welcome return to the top flight.

Four other players also topped 1000 runs that season – Marcus Trescothick (1231) James Hildreth (1147) Cameron White (1083) and Neil Edwards (1039), while the bowling was spearheaded by Andy Caddick with 70 wickets at an average of 24.14 and Charl Willoughby who claimed 62 at 24.68 runs apiece.

Justin Langer can rightfully claim to have been the mastermind behind the most successful period in the Club's recent history. The Aussie arrived in 2006 when Somerset were languishing in the lower reaches of English domestic cricket and during his time at the helm he transformed them into one of the most competitive teams in the country and a force to be reckoned with in any format.

Langer was an inspiration to many of the younger players at the Club including Craig Kieswetter and Pete Trego and in 2010 the season after he left Somerset finished level at the top of the championship, but ended in second place to Nottinghamshire who won one more match.

During his four seasons Langer scored 3535 first class runs at an average of 51.23, which included two triple centuries.

Craig Kieswetter made his championship
debut for Somerset in early May 2007 against
Derbyshire at the County Ground when he made
63 in his first ever innings in the four day format.
From that time the South African-born wicket-
keeper/batsman, who had a Scottish mother,
became ever present in the side and went on to
make his full England debut in early 2010.

In the picture above Kieswetter is 'keeping against
Glamorgan in the penultimate home game of the
season in a game that Somerset won by 299 runs.

In Somerset's first innings Kieswetter set a new
career best for himself of 93, sharing in a ninth
wicket partnership of 130 with Andy Caddick
who made 43 to ensure that the hosts took
maximum batting points.

When he donned the gloves Kieswetter picked
up eight catches during the course of the two
Glamorgan innings.

Left arm bowler Charl Willoughby was no stranger to English conditions when he was signed from Leicestershire before the start of the 2006 season.

The previous year Willoughby took six for 16 when the two sides met at Grace Road and he played against Somerset in the T20 semi final in 2005 at the Oval.

In 2006 the genial South African topped the Somerset championship bowling averages with 66 wickets at 25.56 runs each, he took 23 wickets in List A cricket and 12 in T20 to bring his season's haul to 101.

The following season Willoughby opened the Somerset attack with Andy Caddick in which he took 62 wickets at 24.68 to help bowl Somerset to promotion in the championship.

Opposite, clockwise from top left:
Wes Durston who hailed from Glastonbury and grew up playing through the Somerset age groups
enjoyed a very successful season in 2006.
The all rounder played in 14 championship matches in the season in which he made 765 runs at an
average of 38.35, and claimed 10 wickets at 41.60 each. Here he is seen hitting another boundary
for his home county.

James Hildreth was famous for his scampered singles and here is seen taking off for another during
his innings of 71 against Gloucestershire at the County Ground which Somerset won by an innings
and 76 runs.

During the course of that season Hildreth scored 798 runs in the championship which included 227
against Northamptonshire at Taunton in the final match of the season, making him the youngest ever
double centurion for Somerset.

Keith Parsons enjoyed a successful season in 2006 during which he made 511 first class runs, which
included his career best 153 against Essex at Taunton to take his tally for Somerset beyond 5000 for
the Club, a feat he also achieved in List A cricket.

Below: Cameron White on his way to an unbeaten 116 against Gloucestershire at the County
Ground in the opening T20 fixture of 2006.

Opposite, top from left to right:
Justin Langer made 90 out of an opening partnership of 150 with Cameron White against Gloucestershire in the T20 record-breaking match.

Langer (left) and White on their way to setting the new world record T20 score against Gloucestershire in 2006.

Justin Langer flays another boundary.

Opposite, centre from left to right:
Cameron White hits out – looks like another six from the Aussie.

Cameron White acknowledges his century against Gloucestershire in the T20.

Opposite, bottom from left to right:
Pete Trego (middle) who rejoined Somerset in 2006 carried out the twelfth man duties in the Somerset against Gloucestershire T20 match. Justin Langer is on the left and Cameron White on the right.

Pete Trego is seen here batting against Northamptonshire in the T20 match at the County Ground at the end of June 2007. The man from Weston super Mare hit 20 in this match that the visitors won by the D/L method by 24 runs after the rain brought an early end to proceedings.

Pete Trego was an immediate success when he returned to his home county in 2006. That first season he hit 596 runs in the championship which included 135 against Derbyshire at the County Ground in July.

Players Off the Field

Clockwise from top left: Marcus Trescothick a future Somerset captain enjoying some festive refreshment in front of the Christmas tree in the Colin Atkinson Pavilion in December 2000; Andy Caddick pictured with his wife Sarah and their two children Ashton and Fraser in the Colin Atkinson Pavilion in August 2005; Richard Johnson with Kim Williams, who was the owner of North Gear who sponsored the Somerset shirts in 2005; that's the way to do it – former County Ground favourite Peter Robinson who was a left arm spinner in his playing career shared some of his expertise with Arul Suppiah (left) and Wes Durston in the Centre of Excellence in 2005; James Hildreth signs a young fan's cricket shirt in the Colin Atkinson Pavilion in August 2005, shortly after playing a key role in helping Somerset win the T20 Cup.

Above: In September 2005 it was announced that Ian Blackwell had been appointed captain for the following season and that his vice captain would be Matt Wood (right).

Below: Matt Wood signs a mini cricket bat for a young fan in August 2005.

Above: Marcus Trescothick returns to the County Ground in September 2005 after helping England win the Ashes. The Keynsham-born opening batsman was presented to the crowd during the final home championship match by the Mayor of Taunton Cllr Richard Lees.

Below: Marcus Trescothick pictured with the engraved goblet he was presented with by the Mayor of Taunton after helping England to win the Ashes in 2005.

Ian Blackwell won the Man of the Match Award in the Cheltenham & Gloucester Trophy semifinal against Kent that was played in front of a packed County Ground after scoring 86 in just 53 balls to help the hosts to post 344 for 5.

There were also vital contributions from Mike Burns who made 72 and Peter Bowler with 70.

Kent look well placed in their reply and needed just nine to win off 15 balls with four wickets in hand. However Matt Bulbeck bowled the 49th over and conceded just two runs. Three wickets fell in the penultimate over – two run outs, one for Keith Dutch and the other a spectacular affair by substitute fielder Simon Francis before Bulbeck bowled David Masters with his final delivery.

With six runs needed off the last over Steffan Jones steamed in and had Mark Ealham superbly caught by Dutch off his first ball at mid wicket to send Somerset back to Lord's to defend their C & G title.

Also in the right of the picture is Gianna Tesser who was part of the commercial department at the County Ground for many years.

Top right: Former Somerset captain Mike Burns (third from left) with his wife Carolyn pictured at one of his benefit events with some of the guests including Bob Payne (left), Jason Kerr, Marcus Trescothick and Roy Kerslake.

Centre right: Club President Roy Kerslake presents an engraved silver salver to Peter Bowler in December 2004 in recognition of his contribution to Somerset CCC. Peter is accompanied by his wife Jo.

Bottom right: Somerset fan Simon Trump and his two sons Harry (left) and Jack get to hold the T20 Cup with Carl Gazzard.

Opposite, clockwise from top: Blackacre Farm Eggs were long time supporters of Somerset and in 2005 they sponsored the one day shirts. Ahead of one of the home Totesport League matches the Wurzels played and here Tommy Banner is seen with one of the escaped hens from Blackacre Farm Eggs and Gareth Andrew!; Marcus Trescothick back at the County Ground in September 2005 after helping England to win the Ashes; James Bryant, Keith Dutch, Ian Blackwell and Peter Bowler pictured in 2003; the coveted Twenty20 Cup medal that the Somerset players were presented with after beating Lancashire at the Oval by seven wickets on 30 July.

Above: Keith Parsons signs autographs after another Somerset T20 victory.

Below: Graeme Smith leads the victorious Somerset side off the field. Note the Old Stragglers Bar in the background along with the Ridley Stand and the old pavillion.

Above, left to right: Sam Spurway (left) a wicket-keeper batsman from Ilminster and all rounder Rob Woodman from Taunton both signed contracts with Somerset after graduating through the Academy on 15 August 2005; within a few days of graduating in 2005 Sam Spurway found himself 'keeping for Somerset in the inaugural international T20 competition in Leicester at the end of the season – the youngster from Ilminster made quite an impression when he made his championship debut in August 2006, but then lost his place through injury in early 2007 having played in six first class games and scored 210 runs with a best of 83 and claimed 16 catches behind the stumps; Ian Blackwell pictured with television celebrity Amanda Barrie, a regular visitor to the ground, on the day of the open top bus ride.

Below: Sanath Jayasuriaya proved to be very popular when he spent the afternoon at King's Hall School in Taunton, where in addition to signing autographs the Sri Lankan run scorer took part in a practice match to give the enthusiastic young cricketers a day to remember.

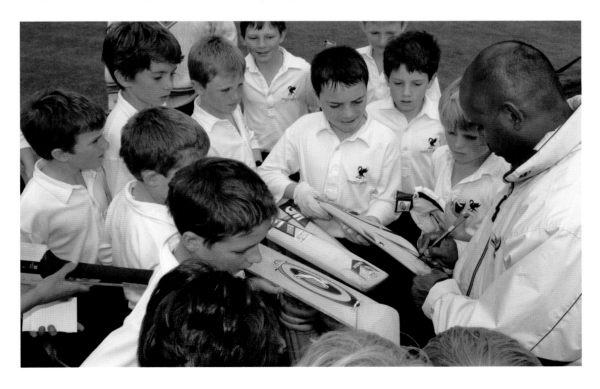

Crowd Scenes at Bath and the County Ground

Above: A timeless scene, the Bath Festival in June 2005 during the Totesport League match between Somerset and Kent.

Opposite, top and centre: The large crowd at Bath enjoy the first day of the championship match against Worcestershire on 8 June 2005.

Bottom: Cricket at The Rec in Bath. Spectators sit around the boundary edge watching Somerset playing Worcestershire in the county championship on 8 June 2005.

Above: Aaron Laraman fielding in front of the Friends of Bath Tent during the Totesport League match between Somerset and Kent in June 2005.

All rounder Laraman joined Somerset from Middlesex in 2003 and between then and the end of 2005 he played in 33 first class matches in which he scored 1019 runs at an average of 29.97 including a best of 148 not out against Gloucestershire at Taunton in 2003.

Laraman also took 59 wickets at 37.61 with a best of five for 58 against Derbyshire at Taunton in 2004.

Left: Cricket at Bath – Somerset regularly played at least one championship and a one day match at the Recreation Ground in Bath, which always looked a picture with the number of tents and the boundary edged with chairs. This picture shows Graeme Smith in Sunday League action against Kent.

Opposite: The crowd gets right behind their Somerset heroes at Bath in June 2005.

Left: Somerset hosted Surrey in the Norwich Union 45 over competition in August 2005. The floodlit match attracted a very large crowd who watched Somerset chase down Surrey's 236 for eight, with four wickets and four overs to spare thanks to 86 from Peter Bowler and 53 from Mike Burns.

Below: A packed house at the County Ground enjoy the 45 over action against Surrey. For a number of years Somerset hosted a floodlit game and it always attracted big crowds.

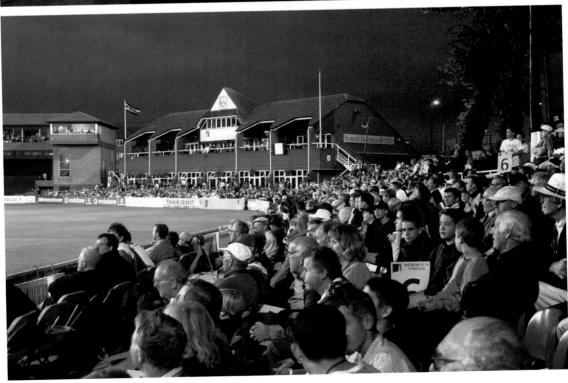

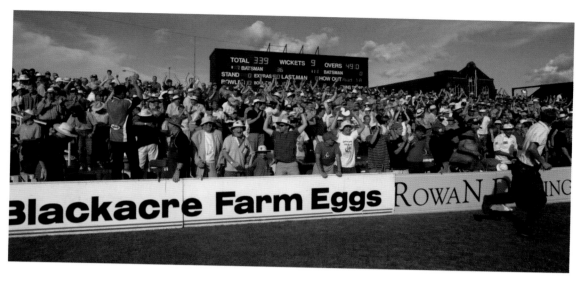

Above: Part of the packed house of 7000 fans celebrate Somerset's Cheltenham & Gloucester Trophy semifinal victory over Kent by five runs in 2002 to see them return to Lord's to defend their title.

In a high scoring game, batting first Somerset made 344 for 5 off their 50 overs, which included 86 off 53 balls from big hitting Ian Blackwell.

When they replied Kent looked well placed at 336 for 6, with two overs to go. However in the penultimate over, bowled by Matt Bulbeck, they scored only two runs and lost three wickets. Two of the wickets were runs outs, one of which by substitute fielder Simon Francis who threw the ball as he dived is still talked about, before Keith Dutch made a superb catch off the first ball of the final over which sparked scenes of jubilation all round the County Ground.

Below: The Somerset fans throng onto the County Ground after watching their heroes pull off a thrilling five run victory over Kent in the Cheltenham & Gloucester Trophy to send Somerset back to their second Lord's final in as many seasons.

Top and centre right: Somerset fans have always been passionate about their one day cricket and here they are seen cheering their local heroes to victory over Australia on 15 June 2005.

Bottom right: A brief shower interrupted proceedings against Australia on 15 June 2005, but thankfully the game carried on and Somerset recorded a memorable victory.

Opposite, top: Christmas comes early at the County Ground – especially if Somerset are winning. This group of wannabee Santas are enjoying their team beating Warwickshire in the 40 over Totesport League in September 2005.

Bottom: A very large crowd enjoyed the thrilling C & G semi-final game between Somerset and Kent that was played at the County Ground on a beautiful day and at the end of which the local heroes were successful and the crowds had to set about booking their tickets for a trip to Lord's – again.

Left: Fans in the Ridley Stand ahead of the start of another home match at the County Ground. This was demolished to make way for Gimblett's Hill.

Below: Somerset fans have always entered into the spirit of the game at the County Ground as a group are shown here in June 2006.

Above: Sitting on the bench seats below the Ridley Stand, which stood on the site where Gimblett's Hill now is situated was a favoured venue by many spectators, old and young.

Below: A packed one day crowd at the County Ground in 2002 when the lime trees still stood in front of the old Barnicotts Building.

Somerset Cricket People

Opposite, top: The young cricketers on the Somerset Academy take a break from their training to enjoy a festive occasion with some of the first team players in December 2004.

Pictured from left to right, back row – Stephen Wheeler, Sam Spurway, Jack Cooper, Liam Lewis, Robin Lett, James Fear and James Fraser.

Middle row – Simon Francis, Matt Wood, Gareth Andrew, John Francis and Rob Woodman.

Front row – Mike Burns (captain SCCC), Colleen Ashbee, Mark Garaway (Academy Director) Jos Buttler and Chris Jones.

Bottom: Andy Nash who was voted in as the new Vice Chairman to work with Giles Clarke at the 2002 Annual General Meeeting.

Below: Giles Clarke shortly after being elected Chairman of Somerset pictured at the County Ground in December 2002.

Bottom: Newly elected Somerset Chairman Giles Clarke and his Vice Chairman Andy Nash face the press soon after taking up their posts with the Club in December 2002.

Above left: Somerset's Head Groundsman Phil Frost spent many years at the County Ground
and during his time in charge of the square won the ECB Groundsman of the Year Award on a
number of occasions. Here he is seen putting the finishing touches to the wicket for the
opening championship match of the season against Derbyshire in April 2004.
Above right: Phil Frost tried many scarecrows to try to keep the seagulls off the wickets
and here he is seen with his latest model in 2002.

Below: Another cup winning team – Head Groundsman Phil Frost with the ECB Award pictured with
Simon Lee (left), Andy Fooks, and his brother Martin Frost.

Top right: We won the Cheltenham & Gloucester Trophy in 2001 – a young Somerset fan comes to terms with the Club's first trophy success for 18 seasons

Bottom right: Former Somerset player Vic Marks who was a member of the team during the Glory Years and is now a member of the BBC Radio Test Match Special Team as well as writing for the *Guardian*.

Bottom left: Richard Gould who was appointed Chief Executive of Somerset in 2005.

Opposite, top: Peter Anderson was the Chief Executive at Somerset County Cricket Club for seventeen years between 1988 and 2005 and during his time at the helm the Club moved forward considerably both on and off the field.

Bottom: Roy Kerslake the President of Somerset CCC pictured on the balcony of the Colin Atkinson Pavilion at the County Ground on the opening day of the championship match against Durham in July 2005.

Right: Somerset's first team scorer Gerry Stickley earned the nickname of Long John Stickley and was suitably attired with a parrot for part of the 2005 season when he was walking with the aid of a crutch. Thankfully by the start of the following season the crutch and the parrot had disappeared!

Below: Alan Whitehead (left) and Merv Kitchen, both former Somerset players umpired the final match of their careers on 25 September 2005 when Derbyshire played at the County Ground in the Totesport League.

Batsman Kitchen played for Somerset between 1957 and 1979 and became a first class umpire in 1982.

Whitehead was a bowler who made his Somerset debut in 1957 and between then and 1961 played in 38 first class matches. He became a first class umpire in 1970 and had thirty-six years on the list.

Above: Recently appointed Chief Executive Richard Gould met up with Somerset Stragglers officials when they hosted MCC at Taunton Vale in 2005. The CEO is pictured with Hugh Duder (left) the Stragglers President and Chairman Mike Giles.

Below: Director of Cricket Brian Rose pictured at the County Ground the day after his team had beaten Australia in a one day match.

Above: Mike Sallis aka Tractor (right) and Paul Bird (centre) both staunch supporters along with another Somerset fan, pictured during the home game against Leicestershire in July 2005.

Left: Former Somerset players Roy Palmer and Mervyn Kitchen who both went on to become very popular and well respected umpires on the First Class list.

Above: Eddie Lawrence (left) being presented with a portrait of himself, painted by Mike Tarr, by Charles Clive Ponsonby-Fane, watched by Tony Stedall, (second left) curator and one of the masterminds of the Somerset Cricket Museum, and Ken Wills, who was also a driving force behind the Museum.

Below: Ken Palmer being presented with a Friends of Bath Cricket Festival tie in June 2005 to mark the 50th anniversary of his Somerset debut at The Rec in 1955. Pictured with the former Somerset all rounder who went on to become a very highly respected first class and Test Match umpire is Derek Brown (left) and Roy Kerslake the Somerset President.

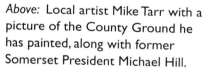

Above: Local artist Mike Tarr with a picture of the County Ground he has painted, along with former Somerset President Michael Hill.

Top right: Smiles all round – Cllr Richard Lees, Mayor of Taunton pictured with Roy Kerslake the President SCCC and Director of Cricket Brian Rose at a reception at the County Ground in early August 2005 to celebrate Somerset winning the T20 Cup.

Centre right: Gianna Tesser and Stevie Rose celebrate Somerset's T20 Cup success in 2005.

Bottom right: Sheila and Tony Stedall who were both very heavily involved in the setting up and running of the Somerset Cricket Museum until they retired in 2006.

Above left: Tony Davies was one of the unsung heroes in the early days of the Somerset Cricket Board. He worked tirelessly behind the scenes as the Chairman of the newly formed SCB before taking on a scouting role for the county across the south west area. *Above right:* Andrew Moulding the first Somerset Cricket Development Officer after the formation of the Somerset Cricket Board became a hugely popular figure in the recreational game in the county and served in the role from 1998 until he retired.

Below: Andrew Moulding (left) along with Tony Davies. Davies was no mean cricketer himself and in the 1950s played on a number of occasions for Somerset Second XI.